NANCY A. BROWN
WWW.VIRTUALGALFRIDAY.COM

Virtual Gal Friday's
VIRTUAL ASSISTANT START-UP GUIDE

Work from Home as a Virtual Assistant!

The Practical, No-Nonsense Approach with Common Sense Advice You Can Use

NANCY A. BROWN
WWW.VIRTUALGALFRIDAY.COM

Virtual Gal Friday's Virtual Assistant Startup Guide

ISBN: 978-1-463789015

©Copyright 2007 thru Current Date - by Nancy A. Brown, All Rights Reserved worldwide under the Berne Convention. May not be copied or distributed without prior written permission -- if you have this book, in electronic or printed form, and didn't pay for it, you are depriving the author and publisher of their rightful royalties.

NANCY A. BROWN
WWW.VIRTUALGALFRIDAY.COM

For permissions, contact info@virtualgalfriday.net

Legal Notices

While all attempts have been made to verify information provided in this publication and accompanying materials, neither the author nor the publisher assume any responsibility for errors, omissions, or contrary interpretations of the subject matter herein. The information contained in this publication is strictly for educational purposes and is not intended for use as a source of legal or accounting advice. The publisher wants to stress that the information contained herein may be subject to varying state and/or local laws or regulations. All users are advised to consult with counsel to determine what state and/or local laws or regulations may apply to the user's particular business.

The purchaser or reader of this publication assumes responsibility for the use of these materials and information. Adherence to all applicable laws and regulations, both federal and state and local, governing professionals licensing, business practices, advertising, and all other aspects of doing business in the United States or any other jurisdiction is the sole responsibility of the purchaser or reader. The Author and publisher assume no responsibility or liability whatsoever on the behalf of any purchaser or reader of these materials. Any perceived slights of specific people, or organizations are unintentional.

NANCY A. BROWN
WWW.VIRTUALGALFRIDAY.COM

NANCY A. BROWN
WWW.VIRTUALGALFRIDAY.COM

Dedication

This book is dedicated to those who have supported me while I built my business.

First to my husband, Larry, and my children Anthony and Alyssa, without you all of my business accomplishments would be nothing.

To my past and current clients, who I have learned so much, working with each of you I was able to develop my skills that allowed me to build my business to the level of success I have reached today.

To my fellow Virtual Assistants, the small handful that created the path for me to follow and those who came after me who were the inspiration for this book.

NANCY A. BROWN
WWW.VIRTUALGALFRIDAY.COM

My Back Story

My story is not much different from those of other Virtual Assistants. The reason I started my business, Virtual Gal Friday, is because I wanted to be home for my children. I was tired of the lengthy commute, and tired of the office politics.

After temping as an administrative assistant and secretary most of the 90's, I knew there had to be an easier way. Once I realized how much the agencies were actually charging and what I was being paid, I knew I had to go out on my own and leave out the middle man!

When I decided to start my business, the thought in my mind was to start a Secretarial Service; I had not yet run into the term "Virtual Assistant". Once I started my research, I found an article posted by Liz Folger of BizyMoms.com and she used the term. After I read her article, I knew she was talking about me and my new business! This was just the beginning of the fledgling VA industry.

It took a couple of years working at night and on weekends to build my business to the level that I could quit my day job and work at it full time. Virtual Gal Friday was operating full time in 1998.

Since then a lot of things have happened. My 2 kids are now both in college! And the VA Industry (and my business) has grown leaps and bounds. Thanks in part to all the great businesses that partnered with myself or

NANCY A. BROWN
WWW.VIRTUALGALFRIDAY.COM

other VA's to really promote the benefits of working with a Virtual Assistant. We can't forget the growth in technology – now with 'working in the cloud' anyone can be Virtual!

NANCY A. BROWN
WWW.VIRTUALGALFRIDAY.COM

Virtual Assistant Start Up Guide

Table of Contents

Chapter 1   11
Do you have the necessary skills and experience?
Working Virtually
Workspace Set Up
Tools You Need to Get Started
Chapter 2   29
Type of Business
Building a Business Plan
Selecting a Business Name
Chapter 3   45
Daily Operations
Policies and Procedures
Emergency Plan
Timing Your Work
Time Management
Invoicing
Chapter 4   77
Develop a Plan
Press Releases
Brochures
Business Cards
Obtaining Clients
Website Basics + Using Wordpress
Chapter 5   113
Facebook
Twitter
Linked In
Chapter 6   119
Code of Ethics
Mission Statements
Client Assessments

Virtual Assistant Start Up Guide

Virtual Assistant Start Up Guide

Chapter 1

Getting Started

- Do you have the necessary skills and experience?
- Working Virtually
- Workspace Set Up
- Tools You Need to Get Started

Getting Started

Important Characteristics Every Entrepreneur Must Have

There are several important traits and values that are common among successful entrepreneurs. Before starting your Virtual Assistant business decide if you have what it takes to be a successful entrepreneur, and a successful Virtual Assistant!

Self Confidence – Success in the highly competitive business world requires confidence and trust in oneself. The world of entrepreneurship is not alien to failure and disappointments. You must have the ability to look within yourself and find the drive to pursue your business goals in this aggressive world. Trust your skills and abilities to push your business to success.

Are You a Risk-Taker? – Trust your instincts and act on them, use that self-confidence of yours and take a chance! Great business ideas sometimes start as an instinct which creative individuals acted upon. There is always the risk of loss in any endeavor, and

Getting Started

entrepreneurs have just the right confidence to take calculated risks to achieve their objective.

When I started my own business, Virtual Gal Friday, I was definitely taking risk. The day I quit my full time job and started my business was scary and wonderful at the same time!

Know the Value of Money and Be Careful about Finances – You must understand the value of money and the cost of things. Typically, successful entrepreneurs learned how to earn and value money at a young age. Most of them started out by earning loose change as teenagers mowing lawns, doing groceries, babysitting for neighbors, etc.

When I was a teenager I babysat for extra money. My Mom also had a daycare center in our home, and I was able to see how a small business was managed from a very young age. I didn't realize it at the time, but my Mom was an entrepreneur herself!

Competitive Spirit – The world of business is a very competitive environment. You should be aggressive enough to pursue your goals despite having many rivals and competitors.

The Virtual Assistant industry is highly competitive, but there always seems to be enough clients and work to go around. Don't be discouraged if a potential client chooses another Virtual Assistant, just push forward and get the next one!

Being honorable with a Good Work Ethic – Although it is a fact that the business world is ruthless; the successful entrepreneur will strive to make every business deal honorable. The mark of a successful entrepreneur lies in a good personal work ethic that ultimately leads to good business practices, excellent reputation and good association with industry peers and business partners.

It's important to have clearly defined Ethic & Mission Statements, see that section in the book for more details.

Know the Importance of Leisure Time – Hard work and determination are very important values every entrepreneur must have. You should also know when it's time to take a step back from all the rigors of business and enjoy some downtime with friends and family. Besides, we all do need a little relaxation to refresh the body and mind before plunging back into the challenging (and stressful) world of business.

Obviously, the characteristics every entrepreneur must have are not limited to the ones in our list. Having these characteristics is not a guarantee that you will be successful; however, they will give you the right ingredients for success.

Do you have what it takes to be a successful Virtual Assistant?

Getting Started

Starting Your Business

Making the decision to start a Virtual Assistant business can be exciting, but this is also a serious step that requires much dedication and hard work. Plan on working very long days during start up, this includes weekends and holidays. Make sure you have the flexibility, commitment and skills/experience to support these working hours.

There are awesome rewards that come from working for yourself and from your own office: no long drives to and from the office, set your own hours, independence, and the fulfillment of managing your own business.

From Virtual Gal Friday:
When I started my business not only did I love working from home; but it allowed me to start homeschooling my two children. That's a priceless reward!

Do you have the necessary skills & experience?

Before starting a Virtual Assistant business you should assess your skills and experience. Having a computer in your home office is helpful, but if you do not know how to utilize your word processing software or put together basic documents you will have a long road ahead of you.

Elance.com offers skills testing. Take the following tests to assess your skills and you will know where your strengths and weaknesses are and this will give you a base to build upon. You do have to sign up as a member to take the tests, signing up is free.

- Spelling
- Vocabulary
- Computer Skills
- MS Excel
- MS Word
- MS Outlook
- Telephone Etiquette
- Office Skills
- Test Your Typing Speed at: TypingtTest.com

The more administrative skills you have, the more prepared you will be for a Virtual Assistant business.

After assessing your skills consider taking take some online courses to gain the administrative skills that you need before proceeding with your business venture. Universal Class (http://www.universalclass.com) is a great place to start.

Never take on a project from a client that you do not have the skills to complete. This will hurt you, your business, and most importantly your client.

Is this for you?

Running a Virtual Assistant business requires self-discipline, determination, focus, perseverance, and hard work. You must also consider that you will be spending a great deal of time on your own and may sometimes feel isolated. There are many Virtual Assistant and home business message boards and online networking groups that will help.

Getting Started

Here is a list of the boards, forums, and groups that I recommend:

- **VA Networking** – vanetworking.com

- **Virtual Assistant Ville** – virtualassistantville.com

- **International Virtual Assistant Association** – IVAA.org

- **Hire My Mom** – hiremymom.com

- **LinkedIn Groups:** You need to be signed up on LinkedIn to join these groups. There are many groups not listed here, you can search groups in LinkedIn to find more that will fit your needs.
    - *American Virtual Assistant Association*
    - *National Association of Virtual Assistants for Coaches*
    - *Virtual Assistant Group*
    - *Creative Online Entrepreneurs*
    - *Executive Secretary Magazine*
    - *Virtual Assistant Tips & Tricks*

Getting Started

Working Virtually

Virtual Assistants are able to work with clients located all over the world and should consider their client's time zones and try to accommodate them. TimeandDate.com will help you keep everything timed correctly. This is especially great when managing your client's calendars and scheduling teleseminars.

Part of working as a Virtual Assistant means you will have multiple clients and that you will need to stay in contact and make yourself available throughout the work day. This not only shows your professionalism, it also shows your client that you are dedicated to their business. Virtual Assistants communicate with clients via email, telephone and instant messaging.

Daily Communication:

Utilizing an instant messenger program like Skype can be helpful. This is a great way to be available to a client without about being tied down to a lengthy phone call, and if you answer phones for clients you can use instant messenger to announce a call before transferring to the client.

Getting Started

Skype is not only for instant messaging - you can also have video chats, share screens and even make phone calls! They even offer apps for various android devices and smart phones.

Receiving Work Items:

Most clients will just email you task lists and documents that need to be worked on. Once you have completed a task that requires sending a file back to a client - you can use a service like YouSendIt.com if the files are over 1 megabyte, smaller files can be emailed.

Not only can you send files via the YouSendIt.com website, they also offer a free add on that works with Microsoft Outlook, that way you just attach to an email and YouSendIt.com does the rest. Be sure to let your clients know that when they need to send you a large file they can go to YouSendIt.com and send to you.

Getting Started

Collaborating with Clients:

It's important to have the ability to collaborate with your clients online, or in the 'cloud'. Setting up <u>Google Docs & Google Apps</u> is a great way to do that. (google.com/apps/intl/en/group/index.html)

The applications you use within Google Apps make a huge difference. You don't have to use alot of apps, keep it simple and then add more apps as you get used to the system.

Not a Google or Gmail fan? Try TeamLab.com they offer a free version and it's a really a great tool for collaboration! TeamLab.com creates a subdomain with your business name in the url.

Here are my recommendations:

- Google Docs - Document Prep and Collaboration
- Google Calendar - Keep your own calendar and access your client's.
- InSightly - Insightly is a great task management tool that connects with your gmail (email) and calendar. You can create tasks directly from your email-

Getting Started

> Download the [InSightly user guide](http://insight.ly/InsightlyForGoogleAppsConceptGuide.pdf) for more information.
> (http://insight.ly/InsightlyForGoogleAppsConceptGuide.pdf)

- Gmail - there are specific settings to have Gmail work with your domain. Coordinate with your webhost to set this up.

Many clients will come to you and already be set up (or partially set up) to work with Google Apps – and depending on the nature of their business, you can either have an account created for you within their Google Apps account (sometimes the easiest way to go) or add your client to your account.

If you decide to collaborate with your client from your account, it's recommended to share docs and tasks, and not give them username/pass with your domain.

When setting up Google Docs on your domain to share documents with your clients go into Settings and select: *"Allow users to use Google Cloud Connect in my Organization and Users can share documents outside this organization."* You and your client will need to

Getting Started

download and install Google Cloud Connect for that feature to work correctly.

There are many great alternatives to Google Apps. Search online using terms 'online file collaboration' or 'online team management' to find the newest and most current available applications. TeamLab.com is a really great alternative and set up is free.

Basically, you want to have a virtual office online that will allow multiple users, file storage, calendar, project and task management and even user forums.

This is a great feature to offer your clients a place to store their projects and to communicate with you daily. You can have 1 account and assign your clients their own user id's. They log in and see their own virtual office workspace.

Having a virtual workspace is not only impressive, it looks professional and shows that you not only care about your business, but you also care about being organized and on task for your clients!

Workspace Setup

Your workspace/office set up will require a few basics to get started: a desk, a good chair, file storage, and a shelf for office supplies. You don't have to spend a lot of money to set up your new office space.

If you do not have a desk, be sure to check local yard sales and eBay for a good 2nd hand desk. You can find affordable desks at Wal-Mart and Target.

If at all possible, a separate room for your workspace/office would work best. A separate space in a corner of a larger room or even a large walk-in closet would make a perfect office area. Whatever space you decide to use; it should be free of outside noise and treated as a traditional office. When you go to work, you are at work and should not be distracted.

Remember, your home office might be tax deductible. Ask your accountant or tax preparer about this deduction.

Getting Started

Necessary Tools

Having a good computer with the right software is crucial to a successful Virtual Assistant business. A computer plus an internet connection is what makes a Virtual Assistant truly virtual because it allows you to work remotely. You will need a good printer, too. Starting out with an All in One is a good idea. (printer/scanner/fax).

Here is a short list of the necessary tools required when starting out as a Virtual Assistant. As your business grows so will your list.

Office Suite Software
- Microsoft Office Professional
- Open Office (openoffice.org)
- Google Docs – this is a GREAT way to collaborate with clients on documents. Just note that the spreadsheets are limited on functionality.

Accounting Software
- QuickBooks
- Peachtree Complete Accounting
- Microsoft Office Accounting Professional

Getting Started

**All recommendations can be found online at:
virtualgalfriday.com/virtual_assistant_services/virtual-assistant-store.html

You will also need a good telephone with a business line, check with your local phone company for a 'distinct ring' line, they will give you a new number that rings through your existing landline and it's a much smaller monthly fee than installing a separate line.

From Virtual Gal Friday:
When selecting software for your business, select the best that fits your budget. This is an investment in your business that will pay you back time and time again.

Virtual Assistant Start Up Guide

Virtual Assistant Start Up Guide

Chapter 2

Business Essentials

- Type of Business
- Building a Business Plan
- Selecting a Business Name

Necessary Steps

Before starting your Virtual Assistant business check with your local zoning office to see how the ordinances in your particular area may affect your business plans. You may need a special permit to operate your business from your home; and you may find that making small changes in your plan will put you into the position of meeting zoning standards.

Many communities grant home occupation permits for businesses that involve typing, sewing and teaching, but turn thumbs down on requests from photographers, interior decorators and home-improvement businesses to be run from the home. And often, even if you are permitted to use your home for a given business, there will be restrictions that you may need to take into consideration. By all means, work with your zoning people, and save yourself time, trouble and dollars.

Obtaining zoning approval for your business, then, could be as simple as filling out an application, or it could involve a public hearing. The important points the zoning officials will consider will center on is how your business will affect the neighborhood. Will it increase the traffic noticeably on your street? Will there be a substantial increase in noise? And how will your neighbors feel about this business alongside their homes?

Choosing a Business Entity

Many people are confused by the different types of business entities. That's why I thought it was important to cover it in this chapter.

You should seek advice from your tax attorney and lawyer before deciding on which form of business entity you need. There are many long term implications to choosing the right or wrong business type, confirm with the professionals before making this important decision.

Sole Proprietorship - A sole proprietorship has many rewards for the small business owner. You control all profits, make all decisions and it is simple to form. The business owner has freedom in regards to business operations. There is also less government restrictions with this type of business entity.

Running a business as sole proprietorship also has some risks, including unlimited liability. If your business is sued, you and your personal assets are at risk. You may have to use your own money or personal loan.

Partnerships - A partnership is an organization of two or more people who contribute to ownership and control over the business.

A partnership is easy to form. It is important that you create a legally binding partnership agreement between all of the partners.

The partnership agreement should include how decisions are made, how the profits should be distributed, how disputes should be resolved, how new partners will be admitted, how existing partners can back out of the agreement, and what steps are necessary to dissolve the partnership.

The advantages for a partnership include its easy formation, profits flowing directly to the owners, benefit of more than one person working the business, and a better chance of raising capital from more than one person.

The disadvantages of a partnership include the liability of all of the partners in case of judgment against the business. Also, the partners are liable for the other partners' actions. Profits of the business have to be shared with other people, disagreements could occur between partners, and the partnership may dissolve on death or withdrawal of one of the partners.

Corporations - A corporation is a state-sanctioned entity that is a separate entity then those who own it. A corporation can be taxed, sued, and it can enter into contractual agreements. A corporation sells shares to its owners who elect a board of directors to oversee the company. A corporation does not dissolve when it changes ownership; it has a life of its own.

Generally, shareholders cannot be held liable for a corporation or its debts, up to their investment in the company. A corporation's officers can be held liable for their failure to perform an action, such as paying taxes. Corporations can raise money by selling stock. A corporation can also deduct the cost of benefits for its officers and employees.

Additionally, a corporation under certain circumstances can elect to become an S Corporation, with similar taxation to a partnership. This election allows shareholders to treat earnings and profits as distributions and have them pass directly to their personal tax returns. The only catch is that if you are an employee, you have to pay yourself "reasonable compensation" for any work you perform for the company.

Disadvantages of a corporation include double taxation for some owners. A corporation is taxed at the corporate level and then again at the personal level for any dividends it pays out. The process to incorporate also takes a lot of paperwork and time, and in most states, money. This process is a lot more complicated than the other forms of business, and it is monitored much more closely by all levels of government.

Limited Liability Company - Limited Liability Companies combine the advantages of corporations of limited liability with the control and tax advantages of a partnership. A Limited Liability Company is more complicated than a normal partnership in its formation.

The owners are the members and the life of the LLC is stated when the forms are filed. In general, the LLC is taxed as a partnership. The advantage of an LLC is the limited liability of its controlling parties.

If the LLC is sued, often times the owners do not have their personal assets at risk. In a general partnership, the owners' assets can be at risk if the company is sued.

The disadvantages include strict IRS rules as to when you can be taxed as an LLC and the rules you need to meet in different states to become an LLC.

Business Plan Basics

This is another topic that confuses many people. Especially when you are just starting out in business and are hear different opinions from everyone on the subject. There are a few rules of thought in regards to the significance of writing a business plan. Many say you should not even consider starting a business without one, and others say that a business plan is not needed. Most agree that it is important to map out a general direction for your business and if you will be applying for funding, a formal business plan is a good idea.

A business plan accurately defines your business, identifies your goals, and serves as your company's resume.

The basic components include a current and pro forma balance sheet, an income statement, and a cash flow analysis. It helps you distribute resources properly, handle unforeseen complications, and make good business decisions.

Because it provides specific and organized information about your company and how you will repay borrowed money, a good business plan is a crucial part of any loan application.

What is a Business Plan Used For?

A business plan is a tool with three basic purposes: communication, management, and planning.

Communication - the business plan is used to attract investment capital, secure loans, convince workers to hire on, and assist in attracting strategic business partners. The development of a comprehensive business plan shows whether or not a business has the potential to make a profit. It requires a realistic look at almost every phase of business and allows you to show that you have worked out all the problems and decided on potential alternatives before actually launching your business.

Management - the business plan helps you track, monitor and evaluate your progress. The business plan is a living document that you will modify as you gain knowledge and experience. By using your business plan to establish timelines and milestones, you can gauge your progress and compare your projections to actual accomplishments.

Planning - the business plan guides you through the various phases of your business. A thoughtful plan will help identify roadblocks and obstacles so that you can avoid them and establish alternatives. Many business owners share their business plans with their employees to foster a broader understanding of where the business is going.

Business Plan Outline

Here is a brief summary of what you should include in your Business Plan.

- **Executive Summary** - Highlights the features of your plan, in 2 pages or less

- **Company Summary** - Company fact page. Company description and history.

- **Products/Services** - Outlines company services/and or products.

- **Market Analysis** - Summarizes typical clients/customers, your competition, and market size/growth potential.

- **Strategy & Implementation** - How you will sell your service, how you will put plan into action, and milestones.

- **Management Summary** - Management team background, experience and accomplishments.

- **Financial Plan** - Important financial elements including sales, cash flow and profits.

The SBA website has a great Business Plan template feature that assists you in writing your business plan.

Check it out here:

http://web.sba.gov/busplantemplate/BizPlanStart.cfm

They also offer a free training course!

http://web.sba.gov/sbtn/registration/index.cfm?courseid=27

Business Essentials

Name Your Business & Website Domain

Naming your business is essential. Take time to name your business and plan it out.

Come up with creative ideas by using websites such as Nameboy.com and Ryhmer.com. Your business name should have high impact and represent your business well. The name of your business is part of your marketing strategy.

Preferably, your business name and website domain name should be the same. After you decide on a business name and domain name, perform a search at the United States Patent and Trademark Office website located: www.uspto.gov/web/trademarks/workflow/start.htm to make sure no other businesses are using the same or similar business name.

Registering a domain name of a company who owns the trademark could result in litigation against you. You could be forced to give up your domain name as well as pay fines.

Business Essentials

Tips for naming your business and web domain:

- Make it memorable
- It should be easy to remember
- Make it unique
- Keep it short
- Easy to pronounce
- Easy to spell
- Consider your target market
- Consider your business image
- Don't limit yourself
- Choose a name that will grow
- Make sure it speaks well, writes well and looks good as a domain name.
- Have a brainstorming session to come up with a list of words associated with your business.
- See what names are working for your competitors

Virtual Assistant Start Up Guide

Chapter 3

Daily Operations

- Policies and Procedures
- Emergency Plan
- Email Accounts
- Setting Up Outlook
- Time Management
- Timing Your Work
- Telephone, Voicemail & Faxing
- Developing Your Service List
- Finding Your Niche
- Setting Your Rates

Daily Operations

Policies and Procedures

Developing policies and procedures will benefit your business and your clients every day. If something happened to you – if you end up in the hospital or worse – could someone step in and keep your business and your projects running smoothly? By putting your policies and procedures in place now, you can prevent a crisis from turning into a catastrophe for your business.

Your Office Policy Manual should include:
- **Mission Statement**
- **Code of Ethics**
- **Emergency Plan**
  - Contact name, phone, and email address of trusted assistant/colleague or friend.
  - Client Contact List with updated email addresses and phone numbers of current clients.
  - Location of backup drive
  - Username/Password and location of account spreadsheet
  - Username/Password of online file storage
  - Username/Password of online office
  - Office Equipment & Software List

Daily Operations

- **Bookkeeping Procedures**
  - Software
  - Invoicing Process
  - Accounts Payable Process
  - Reporting Process
- **Timekeeping Procedures**
  - Software
  - Timing Process
  - Reporting Process (if/when you send to clients)
- **Rates**

  Once you have set your rates keep your rate sheet updated and filed in your Office Policies manual.

- **Proposals**

  Many potential clients will inquire about your services and you will want to present them with a professional proposal. You should have a proposal template created in a word processing program; where you can just update the template with the potential client's name, address and services they are interested in.

- **Contracts**

  It is imperative that you have a work for hire agreement developed for your business. A contract between you and the client protects all parties involved. It should outline services required, rates, payment schedule, cancellation and refund policies.

- **Subcontractors**

    Just as it is important to have a work for hire agreement developed for your clients; you also need a subcontractor agreement in place for any freelancers that you might outsource or partner with.

    - 1099 Form – All Subcontractors should complete and submit back to you for filing at the end of the year.

From Virtual Gal Friday:

At the end of the year use a service like the one that Intuit.com offers to file the 1099's for you. This is also a great service to offer your clients ~ have them send you the W9 forms and you can set up everything in the 1099 system for them, Intuit takes care of the electronic filings with all tax authorities.

Daily Operations

Once you have decided what you will include in your policies and procedures, you can use a template like the one from Klariti.com - www.klariti.com/shop/?hop=nancyvgf - to create the printable version. It's very important to have your **Office Policy Manual** printed out and available in a large binder.

All print outs that are stored in your **Office Policy Manual** should also be saved electronically, stored on a CD and saved with your online backup.

Consider giving a trusted colleague, perhaps a fellow Virtual Assistant, access to your online backups and data – someone you know and trust who could step in and run your business temporarily while you are out. Make sure that this person's name and contact information is listed in your Office Polices manual so that your family or friends can contact them on your behalf. This person can then step in and contact your clients, and keep your work flow running smoothly.

Daily Operations

In Case of Emergency

Don't wait until a crisis to develop an emergency plan. You need to put one in place before opening for business. Saving and backing up your data is critical, not only are you storing your business information, but you will also have work files and other pertinent information from your clients. I recommend using an online file storage / backup like Carbonite. Backup your computer at the very least on a monthly basis.

You might also consider an external drive or a flash drive for your computer, if you choose one of these options be sure to keep the backup off premises in a safe location, like a safety deposit box at your bank. Make sure to include a sheet with all pertinent information in regards to the location of your backup files, the username password for the online backup, and how to access your safety deposit box in your Office Policy Manual.

*Remember that your Office Policy Manual should be stored in 3 ring binder.

Daily Operations

Your Emergency Plan should include:

A spreadsheet with all vital information – password protect this file – update this file often and make sure it's saved to all backups. This file should include all usernames and passwords to anything requiring them. Keep the password and file location of this spreadsheet in your Office Policy Manual.

Make a list of all your office equipment that you will need to take with you if you evacuate to keep your business running smoothly. Keep this list in your Office Policies Manual, and saved in all backups.

Keep your current client files organized and in a handy place if you need to grab them and run. Keep portable plastic file boxes on hand so that you can store files and carry with you. This is actually what I use for all client files. Depending on the amount of paperwork you have for each client, you can usually fit 2-3 clients per file box. All printed documents pertaining to the Emergency Plan should be slipped into sheet protectors. Keep your Office Policy Manual up to date and in a convenient location to grab it and go.

Email Accounts

Since communication is key to any successful Virtual Assistant practice, having a working email address and software like Microsoft Outlook© is equally important.

If you have registered your domain name and set up web hosting you should have free email addresses that go with that hosting account. Ask your web hosting provider about creating email addresses in the control panel area of your web hosting account. I recommend HostGator.com (http://bit.ly/vghost) for all webhosting needs, and GoDaddy.com (http://bit.ly/vgfdomain) for registering your domain names.

You can have your domain name registered and web hosting set up *without* having a complete website online, it's a necessity to having a professional email address. The main thing is to have the domain name and hosting account so that you can create email addresses.

*Note, webhosting accounts control the email addresses, if you are working with Google Apps; there

Daily Operations

are special settings that need to be adjusted to utilize your email through Google Apps (Gmail). Be sure to contact your hosting provider for assistance. I actually use both, I have used Microsoft Outlook© for many years, and I use Google Apps with some of my email addresses to utilize the tools we discussed earlier. You can download your email to Microsoft Outlook© and still save it in Gmail.

Even though you can use an email address associated with a free service such as Yahoo or Hotmail, it doesn't put forth a professional image like an email address associated with your own domain would do. The email name marysmith@virtualassistant.com would a have more professional impact than marysmith@yahoo.com, and never use cutesy free email names for professional emails, kitten85@hotmail – is not professional and could leave a bad first impression on potential clients.

Microsoft Outlook© Tips

Email correspondence, especially in business, is an essential form of communication and should meet the same standards as any other form of written communication. Keeping this in mind, it's a good idea to proofread your emails before clicking that 'send' button.

Follow the steps below in Microsoft Outlook© (2003 and 2007) to automatically spell-check your emails before they are sent:

- Click on: Tools - Options - Spelling –
- Check the 2nd checkbox,
- "Always check spelling before sending" - OK

Email Signatures

Including your signature with outgoing messages makes your email look more professional, and it's a great way to market your business!

- Tools – Options - Select the "Mail Format" tab – click "Signatures"
- Enter a name for your new template - Select start from a blank signature – Next
- To add a letterhead to your message template - Right Click within the Signature Text Edit Area - select "Insert Image"
- Find the image you want to use - modify the layout to set the alignment to 'top' –OK.
- To add text to the signature, then add the text below the letterhead image, on the signature text edit area. You can also add a link to your site, by selecting the text above which the link will apply, then right click and choose - Edit Hyperlink
- When you are done, click Finish.

Email Rules

Creating rules that sort your email as it is downloaded into your inbox is another feature of Microsoft Outlook© that keeps your email organized. This really helps when you have multiple clients, multiple projects and multiple email addresses. If you are only using Gmail - you can still use this system but instead of setting up in folders, you will create labels and filters to organize your emails.

Start by creating folders in your inbox.
- New – Folder – Right Click in the box and type the name you want for that folder, for example: clients – or inquiries. You can also create new folders from within the Rules Wizard.

Creating Rules

- Mail - Tools - Rules and Alerts - New Rule.
- Click Start from a blank rule, and then click Next.
- Under Select when messages should be checked, select Check messages when they arrive or Check messages after sending, and then click Next.

Daily Operations

Create a rule based on a name or subject
- Open the message you want to base a rule.
- Tools – Rules & Alerts
- Select the conditions and actions you want to apply.

Create a rule based on a folder
- Open the folder that contains the message.
- Right-click the message you want to base a rule.
- Click Create Rule.
- Select the conditions and actions you want to apply.

Junk Mail Filter

Outlook will send junk mail directly to the Junk E-Mail folder. All email that is considered to be junk will be put in the Junk E-mail folder. To change the settings of your junk email filter, just go to your Inbox, click Actions, then Junk E-mail, and then Junk E-mail options.

There are four settings for the Junk mail filter as described below:

1. *No Automatic Filtering* – No filtering - Blocked senders will still be put in the Junk E-mail folder.
2. *Low* - Default Setting. The most obvious junk will be filtered.
3. *High* - This setting will catch most of the incoming junk, but might also catch some legitimate emails, so be careful! Check your Junk E-mail folder occasionally for email that has been sent there by mistake; however, you can add those senders to your trusted senders list to prevent them from being considered as junk in the future.

Daily Operations

4. S*afe Lists Only* - The most restrictive setting possible. The only email you will receive will be from people or domains in your Contacts list or on your trusted senders list.

From Virtual Gal Friday:
You can apply these instructions to Gmail. Instead of creating rules, you can use 'labels' and 'filters' to sort your inbox and organize your mail into folders.

Daily Operations

Time Management

Project & Task Management is essential working as a Virtual Assistant, since you will be handling multiple projects for multiple clients at one time. Project management software with task management features like **Insightly** (thru Google Apps) or **TeamLab.com** are ideal. If you will be using Freshbooks.com for invoicing, they offer a built in timer and task management tools that work great!

Here are some tips to help you with your daily time management:

Use a timer – Pick one task on your task list, set your timer for 15 minutes and start working. Don't worry about finishing; just get started on the task. Attacking tasks in small increments helps you stay focused.

Delegate – Solicit the help of others to complete time consuming projects. Subcontracting other Virtual Assistants to help with data entry and telephone answering is a good way to create more time for you to work on other projects.

Daily Operations

Set goals – Set a long term goal, then set the short term goals that will get you there.

Sort mail immediately – you will either, trash it, take action or file it. Try not to touch it more than once. If you need to take action be sure to trash it or file it after.

Use Voicemail – Let your phone go to voicemail while you are working so you don't break concentration during a project.

Use checklists - For tasks that are dealt with on a regular basis, create simple checklists so that you don't miss a step.

Organize - A place for everything, and everything in its place. Organize your workspace so that everything has a home. It will make locating and storing things much easier.

Prepare - Set aside 5 minutes at the end of your day to review your checklist & tasks for the next day.

Timing Your Work

It doesn't matter if you bill your client by the hour or by the project, it's a good idea to utilize a time tracking tool for everything that you work on for each client.

For the per project clients, those you bill a flat fee for a project like web design or graphic work you should still time your work as this will help you when determining your rates for future projects. For the per hour clients, using time tracking software is an essential part of the billing process. You should be tracking everything you do for every client on a daily basis.

There are many time tracking software options on the market, many are free and simple to use, and others are more complex and costly. TimeStamp by Syntap (http://www.syntap.com) is free and very simple to use. You can save as many project files as needed. It's a good idea to create a folder for each client and start a new project file each month, or at the beginning of each billing cycle for each client.

Daily Operations

If you email your time report to your client each month with their invoice, you might want to save the timestamp report in pdf format. It looks clean and emails well. As mentioned earlier, Freshbooks.com also offers a task timer; it works great and immediately logs time into timesheets that you can later associate with client invoices. You can also copy your time from your other timers into your Freshbooks.com timesheets.

From Virtual Gal Friday
I have used several timing software programs through the years, paid and free. But, I always go back to TimeStamp by Syntap.com, it's small, and easy to use.

Daily Operations

Telephone/Voicemail/Fax Tools

A very important part of any Virtual Assistant business is telephone, fax and voicemail tools. Check with your local telephone company to see what options they offer. It's a good idea to set up unlimited long distance for outgoing calls, many clients will be located all over the country and if you will be placing calls on their behalf this will save money.

Even though you more than likely have a cell phone, it's a good idea to keep a landline desk phone as your office phone. You should also have separate phone lines for business and personal; it keeps things separate and allows your business to remain professional.

Many phone companies offer distinct ring lines, they will give you a separate phone number for each line and it will actually ring to your existing main number but with a double or triple ring. If you are able to set up a distinct ring line, do it. It's a lot cheaper than a traditional second line.

Daily Operations

Once you have a second line (either distinct ring or traditional) you can then set up your virtual number for your business. There are many services online now offering toll free numbers for a very reasonable monthly fee. Ringcentral www.ringcentral.com - offers great packages for toll free numbers, voicemail and fax. All voicemails and faxes can be sent to you via email.

What's really great about a service like this one is you are allowed a certain number of extensions based on the package you purchase. You can assign extensions to different departments of your business. If you will be answering phones for clients, you can also set up a toll free number and assign an extension for each client, and when it rings to your office you know exactly how to answer the call based on the caller id that shows on your phone. You can also use extensions as dictation or voicemail only lines, many clients just want to send you a quick message about a task and if you give them a specific extension to call you for this they can leave a message for you anytime night or day. It works great!

Faxing from your office sometimes requires a stand-alone fax machine, so you might want to consider purchasing an all in one printer (printer, copier, fax) for

Daily Operations

those times. However, for most faxing you should be able to utilize the virtual fax that comes with your virtual phone number system. You can even send out faxes with your regular email client (like Outlook) just by using the send to number as the email recipient, www.ringcentral.com does offer this feature, make sure to read their help file for specific email to fax instructions.

From Virtual Gal Friday:
I don't see anything wrong with using your cell phone for outgoing calls and even incoming calls – keep in mind you want to appear professional at all times. Do dropped calls and garbled conversations come across as professional?

If you live in an area where that happens frequently opt to keep your landline.

Daily Operations

Developing Your Service List & Finding Your Niche

One of the first things you need to do when setting up your Virtual Assistant business is to decide on what services you will offer. Here is a list of services that will help you develop your own. *Remember that this is a basic list – create your list based on your skills.*

- Word Processing
- Data Entry
- Database Development
- Spreadsheets
- Bookkeeping
- Desktop Publishing
- Telephone Answering
- Email Management
- Customer Service Assistance
- Calendar Management
- Appointment Scheduling
- Blog Maintenance
- Travel Plan Assistance
- Printing
- Web Design
- Ebook Formatting & Setup
- Article Submissions
- Search Engine Optimization
- Marketing
- Social Media Management
- Real Estate Assistance
- Medical Office Assistance
- Legal Office Assistance

Consider a 'niche' or specialty service that will allow your expertise and skills to shine. You will enjoy your work every day because you will be working with clients in the industry you are most interested in.

Ask yourself the following questions:

- What are my hobbies?
- What interests me?
- Which existing clients do I enjoy working with most? Why? In which industries do they work?
- Define your ideal client

Once you have answered these questions you will soon see a pattern and this will allow you to focus in on your niche. Now go through your list of services and remove the ones that:

- you don't enjoy.
- aren't profitable.
- aren't requested.

By taking these small steps you will be closer to defining your niche as a Virtual Assistant.

Setting Your Rates

Virtual Assistants usually charge by the hour. Rates range from $15 - $75 per hour, based on expertise and the difficulty of the task. Many Virtual Assistants work with clients on a retainer, this means they are paid up front and the client sends work when needed.

Some Virtual Assistants offer 'carry over' credit for unused time to retainer clients, and others do not. This is a decision you will need to make for your business. If you decide not to carry unused hours over, be sure your clients understand this and make it a part of your contract terms.

New Virtual Assistants often underestimate the value of their services. The more specialized your service is, the more you may be able to charge for those services.

Visit fellow Virtual Assistant websites to see what they are charging for similar or the same services.

Use the worksheet located here to figure your hourly rate: http://www.ninafeldman.com/resources/pricing-worksheet

Find Your Billable Hours & Operating Costs to Calculate your Hourly Rate

Once you have calculated your Hourly Rate, compare it with your competitors. If it's too high, you will need to lower it and make some adjustments to your available billable hours and operation expenses, as well as desired profit to assure your business does make a profit.

Consider your target market before setting your rates. If you target business executives, then naturally you could charge them more than you could college students.

- Price your services according to supply and demand

If you provide specialized services and the demand is high but the supply of Virtual Assistants offering the same services is low, you can charge more for those services. On the other hand, if the supply is high, you may want to consider more competitive rates.

Daily Operations

EXAMPLE PROPOSAL/CONTRACT FORM
(Email me for a working copy of this example: info@virtualgalfriday.net)

THIS IS NOT TO BE TAKEN AS LEGAL ADVICE, AS ALWAYS YOU SHOULD ALWAYS SEEK ADVICE OF A QUALIFIED ATTORNEY. THIS IS FOR EXAMPLE PURPOSES ONLY.

Attention: Mr. John Smith
CLIENT NAME
ADDRESS
PHONE
EMAIL

Dear Client Name,

COMPANY NAME is pleased to present this proposal to your company for **Virtual Office Management Services** including:

EXAMPLE LIST – UPDATE TO REFLECT YOUR SERVICES AND THE SERVICES THE CLIENT REQUESTED
- Virtual Office Assistance and Management
- Phone answering/Follow Up Phone Calls
- Appointment Scheduling & Confirmations
- Website Maintenance (as/if needed)

We have all of the skills, software and equipment to fulfill your company's Virtual Assistant needs.

Based on the descriptions provided and the time to fulfill these tasks on a monthly basis we recommend either of the following monthly packages:

1. Virtual Office – X hrs per month - $X00
2. Virtual Office - X hrs per month - $X00

** disclaimer here – example: Monthly payments are retainer payments and paid upfront each month. Unused hours will carry over for a max of 3 months.

Thank you for the opportunity to submit this proposal. I hope that you will find COMPANY NAME HERE to be the perfect VA practice to accommodate your needs. Please feel free to contact me via phone or email to answer any questions that you may have.

YOUR SIGNATURE HERE – USE A GRAPHIC FILE OF YOUR SIGNATURE

Your Name
Company Name
Email address | website url
City, State, Zip
Phone
Fax

Daily Operations

(logo here)
**COMPANY NAME
YOUR NAME
WORK FOR HIRE AGREEMENT**

This Work for Hire Agreement ("Agreement") is made this **DATE** , between **YOUR NAME, COMPANY NAME** having its principal place of business at **ADDRESS, CITY, STATE, ZIP USA** and
xxx
In this Agreement, the party who is contracting to receive the services shall be referred to as the "Client" and the party who will be providing the services shall be referred to as the "Contractor".

1. DESCRIPTION OF SERVICES. Beginning on **DATE** - Contractor will provide
the following services (collectively, the "Services"):

Virtual Office Administration/Management

- UPDATE TO FIT YOUR SERVICE LIST

PAYMENT FOR SERVICES. Monthly Retainer: (select one)

☐ Virtual Office – X hrs per month - $X00
☐ Virtual Office - X hrs per month - $X50

a) Payments are retainer payments and paid up front.
b) **Contract retainer payments are non-refundable.** NO EXCEPTIONS.
c) Monthly invoices and time for previous work cycle will be submitted to client via email monthly and client will be provided a secure link to access invoice and to make a payment via credit card or paypal.
d) Payments are considered 'late' after 7 days and all work will cease until payment is made after the 7th day. See termination clause (#5) for more details.

3. INVOICING POLICIES. All invoices after the initial invoice will include any previously authorized expenses, and overages. (retainers only)

1. Contractor will notify client of possible overages and wait for authorization to exceed approved hours if needed. Overages will be billed at the same hourly rate as set forth in the agreement.
2. Client will reimburse contractor for approved expenses – such as postage, paper, envelopes, long distance, etc.

5. TERM/TERMINATION. This Agreement shall commence on Month Day, Year- and shall expire 1 year from this date.

Contractor agrees to perform services for the Company on or before the expiration of the term set forth above. Jkl908bnm

This Agreement may be terminated by either party upon 30 days written notice to the other party. Email is acceptable. Company will pay Contractor any fees due upon written notice of termination.

Daily Operations

Any overages or payments due to Contractor at time of termination must be paid within 7 days of termination notice. If payment is not made Contractor by the 7th day, the Contractor will have the right to start collection activities against the Company.

6. RELATIONSHIP OF PARTIES. It is understood by the parties that Contractor is an independent contractor with respect to Client and not an employee of Client. Client will not provide fringe benefits, including health insurance benefits, paid vacation, or any other employee benefit, for the benefit of Contractor.

7. WORK PRODUCT OWNERSHIP. Any copyrighted works, or other ideas, discoveries, inventions, patents, products, computer code or other information (collectively, the "Work Product") developed in whole or in part by Contractor in connection with the Services shall be the exclusive property of Client. Upon request, Contractor shall sign all documents necessary to confirm or perfect the exclusive ownership of Client to the Work Product.

8. CONFIDENTIALITY/NONDISCLOSURE. Contractor will not at any time or in any manner, either directly or indirectly, use for the personal benefit of Contractor, or divulge, disclose, or communicate in any manner any information that is proprietary to Client. Contractor will protect such information and treat it as strictly confidential. This provision shall continue to be effective after the termination of this Agreement. Upon termination of this Agreement, Contractor will return to Client all records, notes, documentation and other items that were used, created, or controlled by Contractor during the term of this Agreement.

9. ENTIRE AGREEMENT. This Agreement and the aforementioned Non Disclosure Agreement contain the entire agreement of the parties, and there are no other promises or conditions in any other agreement whether oral or written.

10. SEVERABILITY. If any provision of this Agreement shall be held to be invalid or unenforceable for any reason, the remaining provisions shall continue to be valid and enforceable. If a court finds that any provision of this Agreement is invalid or unenforceable, but that by limiting such provision it would become valid and enforceable, then such provision shall be deemed to be written, construed, and enforced as so limited.

Party contracting services:

Printed Name:_____

By: _____
Signature & Date – *by signing this agreement I am stating that I have read and fully understand and agree with all terms.*

Service Provider:
Printed Name: **YOUR NAME PRINTED**

By: ***YOUR SIGNATURE FILE HERE*** DATE

Invoicing

Retainer clients should be billed monthly, and hourly clients should be billed every 2 weeks.

Using an online system like FreshBooks.com (http://bit.ly/qRjI4Q) makes invoicing very easy and it works with PayPal and other payment services. They also offer project management tools, a task timer, and reporting.

Whatever invoicing tool you use, be sure to include your time on the invoice. Even if you are on a retainer with a client, it's important to include all time used.

Clients like to see where their money is being spent. If you are keeping good track of your time, as we discussed earlier, this will not be a problem to copy/paste your time into the invoice. If you are using the FreshBooks.com timer, you can import time right from the timer into your client invoice.

Daily Operations

<u>Invoices should include the following:</u>

Your Company Details (name, email, address, phone)

Client Details (name, email, address, phone)

Payment Methods Accepted, if you take PayPal or another electronic method be sure to include a hyperlink so it's easy for them to pay your invoice.

A line that clearly states payment terms such as:

- Payment Due Upon Receipt
- Payment Due by (Date)
- If any credits will be carried over, be sure to list those.

The first line of the invoice should show the total hours being billed such as:

| Virtual Assistant | 10 Hours | $25 | $250 |

- The second line of the invoice should reflect all itemized time such as:

Time Worked August 2011:	
8/1 – Newsletter Design –	1
8/5 – Data Entry, Add Newsletter Subscribers	1
8/6 –Mail Merge Letters – 200 Letters – Print & Mail	2
8/10 – Phone Call with Client	1
8/15 –Reminder Calls to Customers	1
8/22 – Bank Reconciliations	2

Chapter 4

Marketing Your Business

- Develop a Plan
- Press Releases
- Brochures
- Business Cards
- Obtaining Clients
- Website Basics + Using Wordpress

Developing a Plan

Developing a successful and profitable Virtual Assistant business requires a long term vision, planning and patience. Having a plan to follow to accomplish your long term goals is imperative if your planned success is to become a reality.

Think about where you want to be and what you really want to be doing within your Virtual Assistant business in the next 3 years. We suggest 3 years because that is a realistic amount of time to expect large changes to take place. Many of your goals may take longer than 12 months to achieve (we all know how quickly a month can pass us by!).

What do you want to achieve in 3 years?

What is your motivation for these goals?

Because you 'want' these goals or they are something you 'think' you should achieve?

When deciding on goals, make sure they are on your list for the right reasons. Rule out goals that you have set for yourself that do not line up with your values and dreams.

FOCUS ON WHAT YOU REALLY WANT!

Aim High! By playing safe you will be selling yourself short, or simply planning not to fail. No one sets out to fail, it is okay to take calculate risks to reach new levels in your business.

Consider using a vision board - (http://yep.it/vgvision) to help you 'visualize your goals'.

How Will You Get There? No matter what your long term goals are, you need to plan out how you are going to reach those goals. Let's say you are currently making $40k a year and hope to reach the $100k in 3 years, you have to decide on the changes you will make to reach that goal. Outline the steps and amount of time that you will need to take to move ahead in achieving these goals.

What Do You Need to Get There?

Branding - Establish a clearly defined brand for your business, which you can use from this point forward as the foundation for literally all of your business decisions to follow.

Copywriting Skills - Learning how to write effective sales copy save you time and expense on your promotions. That's true if you write your own copy or outsource this task.

Direct Marketing - This will allow you to reach a wider audience, and you will learn the nuances of sales psychology that cause your prospects to act quickly.

Additional Training - Make sure to list all skills that you need to improve upon. Universal Class is a great place to start for affordable training and tutorials.

Assess Your Goals - Which goals are realistic to achieve? Which are doable? And which aren't? If you need to learn a lot of new skills, how much time can you dedicate to doing so? Can you afford training?

1 Year Plan - Starting with the longer 3 year plan allows you to visualize the goals you truly want to achieve. It also allows you to see the considerable progress you can make. You will also need to build some short-term steps that will lead the way to your 3-year goals. Outline the goals that you would like to achieve in each 1 year timeframe.

Plan It Out - Creating an outline of tasks for each yearly plan is a really effective way to stay on task with your goals. Your outline should include a timeline of your goals and how you will achieve them.

Example Plan:

Website by November 1st

- Hire a web designer by September 1st
- Start Social Media / Networking by October 1st
    - Enlist Social Media Specialist for Assistance
    - Sign Up with Facebook, Twitter, LinkedIn by October 15th
    - Research Webhosting, set up webhosting by October 1st
    - Website draft due for review by October 1st
    - Changes back to web designer by October 5th
    - All final changes completed and ready for final review by October 15th
    - SEO and website submission before October 31st
    - Website 'live' November 1st

Add the 1-year plan to your calendar. Microsoft Outlook Calendar or Google Calendar both work great. You should add an appointment to your calendar for each of the key milestones in your plan, and work hard to keep them.

Stay on Schedule. If you miss an appointment, adjust your schedule to finish that task or goal. Remember that most of the smaller tasks are all leading to the larger goal in your plan. If you miss one task; that task must be completed before moving on and completing that goal. In our example above if we miss the website changes due date that will put the web designer behind and possibly miss the launch date of November 1st. Missing one of the smaller tasks will affect the larger goal.

Publicity Tips

By utilizing the internet you can perform a variety of free techniques that will bring potential clients to your website and grow your business. The most effective methods are: social media, article marketing, blogging, search engine optimization, networking and press release distribution.

Article Marketing - Writing useful and informative articles and submitting to article directories and websites in your niche market will help establish you as an expert online and is a great way to get free exposure for your business. Each article you submit should contain your bio and a link back to your website for maximum exposure.

Example: About the Author

Jane Smith is a Virtual Assistant who works with speakers and authors. To read more about Jane, visit her website: http://www.yourvasitehere.com

Here is a short list to get you started with your article submissions:

EzineArticles.com
GoArticles.com
ArticleDashboard.com
SearchWarp.com
ArticlesBase.com
iSnare.com
Buzzle.com
ArticleCity.com
IdeaMarketers.com
ArticleAlley.com

Start a Blog - You can blog about your services, include helpful tips, research new software and write a review, the options are endless! You can include articles that you have written for article marketing. If you use WordPress to develop your website, you can include your blog with your website. (see 'Website Basics' for more information)

Optimize Your Website - Optimizing your website for the search engines is how clients searching sites like Google and Yahoo find your business. (see 'Website Basics' for more information)

Social Networking Online- Use networking sites like Facebook, Twitter, and LinkedIn to name a few, to reach your target market. Join online forums and professional associations to network with fellow Virtual Assistants.

Start a Mailing List – Stay in touch with clients, potential clients, and anyone else who visits your website by starting a mailing list. Sign up with one of the many auto responder services such as Mailchimp.com, AWeber.com, 1ShoppingCart.com or ConstantContact.com. No matter which one you choose, they all provide you with the html code for your signup form that you can place on your website or blog. When a visitor fills out their information, they'll be automatically added to your mailing list. You can send out mailings to announce specials, new services, new product promotions and lots more.

Media Kit

A media kit showcases key elements about your company, what you do, who you are and why it's important to a potential client.

You should have your media kit prepared in advance for mailing to media outlets and potential clients. You never know when you will meet a potential client and keep plenty on hand for networking events. Having a media kit to hand to them will make certain they remember you and your business.

It's not necessary to spend a lot of money on expensive materials; the most important thing is that you portray a professional image. A basic media kit should include, at the very least, a well written cover letter, a brochure, a press release, business cards and information about your company's history and your mission.

Your media kit should be kept in a high quality, professional presentation folder. Folders with die cuts for a business card are perfect for media kits. A label with your company information or logo placed on the front will further personalize your media kit.

Consider including your newsletter (if you have one) and any articles you have written (remember the article marketing we discussed earlier).

Don't forget to make follow up phone calls 3-4 days after your media kit has been mailed out. Keep your media kit updated and send out a new one each quarter to media and advertising contacts.

Press Releases

You can generate free publicity by writing a press release. Press releases should be included in your media kit and also sent via email/fax or regular mail to media outlets, such as newspapers, magazines, and even radio and television stations. You should also distribute them online (see list below) to increase your exposure.

Places to submit your press releases for free and to read existing press releases:

i-newswire.com
prlog.org
24-7pressrelease.com
free-press-release.com
pr9.net
prfree.com
1888pressrelease.com
addpr.com
pr.com
malebits.com
pressreleasepoint.com
newswiretoday.com

Marketing Your Business

Press releases all follow a basic outline, as shown:

###

FOR IMMEDIATE RELEASE:
CONTACT: Contact Person Name
Company Name
Voice Phone Number
FAX Number
Email Address
Website URL

Jane's Virtual Assistant Services,. Announces Addition of Telephone Answering to their List of Virtual Office Services

This headline is one of the most important components of the press release – you want to grab the attention of the reader/editor. It should be in **bold type** and use a font that is larger than the body text. Ideal fonts are Arial, Times New Roman, or Verdana. Keep the headline to 80-125 characters max. Capitalize every word with the exception of "a", "the" "an" or any word that is three characters or less.

<City>, <State>, <Date> - The first paragraph of your press release should be written in a clear and to the point manner. Keep the opening sentence to 25 words or less. Never assume that the reader has read your headline. It needs to contain information that will "attract" the reader. Your story must be newsworthy and factual; don't make it a sales letter or it will end up in the garbage.

Answer the questions "who", "what", "when", "where", "why" and "how". Your press release should include pertinent information about your product, service or event. If writing about a product, make sure to include details on when the product is available, where it can be purchased and the cost. If you're writing about an event, include the date, location of the event and any other pertinent information. You should include a quote from someone that is a credible source of information; include their title or position with the company, and why they are considered a credible source.

Keep your sentences and paragraphs short; a paragraph should be no more than 3-4 sentences. Your release should be between 500 to 800 words, written in a word processing program, and spell checked for errors. Don't forget to proofread for grammatical errors. The mood of the release should be factual, not hyped; don't use a sales pitch as it will ruin your credibility with the reader.

Marketing Your Business

The last paragraph before the company information should read: For additional information on (put in the subject of this release), contact "name" or visit www.website.com. If you offer a sample, copy or demo, put the information in here. You can also include details on product availability, trademark acknowledgment, etc. in this area of the release.

ABOUT JANE'S VIRTUAL ASSISTANT SERVICES - Include a brief description of your company along with the products and services it provides. ###

Marketing Your Business

Brochure & Business Card Basics

Printed materials such as brochures and business cards should be included with your media kit. You should also have your brochure saved in PDF format and available for download from your website, or ready to email to a potential client after you have received their initial inquiry.

When creating your brochures you should work on the copy first. Because you will only have a certain amount of space available. Once your copy is finished, you can place graphics (including your logo) to reinforce your message.

Continue the look and feel of your website into your brochure, this creates consistency and develops your corporate branding/image. You can set up your brochure in MS Word or Publisher – find free templates on the Microsoft website; you can even print them yourself!

Many office supply stores stock brochure quality paper. If you are worried about printing yourself, there are many online companies that will allow you to upload your designed brochure and they print and ship to you for reasonable rates.

Business cards are very useful in marketing your business and they can be used many ways. They must be included in your media kit, as well as any mailings to clients.

Your business card should be easy to read, do not use a font smaller than 10 point for your primary information. The most important information to include on your card is: company name, phone number, email address and web site URL.

Keep your card design consistent with your website and brochure and other marketing materials. Make your card memorable by using elements that cause your card to stand out. You can use fold–over cards to create mini–brochures or include your photo on your card. For free templates visit the Microsoft website. If you are setting up basic business cards you can purchase business card stock and print your business cards on your office computer. Professional printers like Overnight Prints (http://bit.ly/pXYheM) offer a wide variety of card stock and printing options.

Getting Clients

Based on your marketing efforts many clients will find you by visiting your website and other advertising methods that you use. You will receive phone calls and emails inquiring about your services based on these efforts. However, it may take time for your website traffic to increase and for your branding efforts to gain recognition for your business. During this phase there are alternative methods you can use to connect with potential clients.

Start with current or former employers. Provide them with your media kit and set up a meeting. The positive to marketing to this group is that they are already familiar with you, your skills and the quality of work you provide.

Sign up with the International Virtual Assistant Association at http://www.ivaa.org, and watch the RFP's. There are a 2 other Virtual Assistant websites worth mentioning that will lead you not only to finding clients, but networking with Virtual Assistants as well.

Marketing Your Business

VA Networking – vanetworking.com

The forums and signing up is free, but they also offer some monthly membership packages. Using the url included above will take you to the sign up for the "Get Clients" package that will give you access to the job postings.

VirtualAssistantVille – virtualassistantville.com
This website does charge a nominal fee to have your business listed and to have access to the RFP's.

Job boards and search engines are also great places to start. Both will allow you to find clients who need help by using specific keywords.

Hire My Mom - hiremymom.com - is a GREAT job/career directory, they do charge a fee but the work is real and new projects are posted daily.

Marketing Your Business

Example Keywords (be sure to use the quotation marks as show, this will search on the complete phrase):

"Virtual Assistant"	"freelance job/s"
"virtual secretary"	"1099 Contractor"
"administrative assistant remote"	"Virtual Assistant"
	"remote office"
"remote contractor"	"1099 employee"
"home office required"	"virtual worker/employee"
"independent contractor"	"online work"
"freelancer"	"telework"
"freelance"	

***Be very careful when answering ads on Craigslist,**

<u>NEVER</u> sign up for work that involves you cashing a large check or money order, and sending cash via western union to someone. This is a classic scam and you will get burned.

Freelance websites such as guru.com, odesk.com, and elance.com allow freelancers to bid on projects posted by clients. If your bid is accepted you will be awarded the project. Most of these projects are short-term, but

Marketing Your Business

are a great way to build your clientele and your portfolio.

Even though there are legitimate free 'work at home websites', be cautious because these leads are sometimes outdated and many others have probably also submitted their interest in the positions available. Be sure to research the job leads for authenticity.

You can also have some flyers printed and pass them out to local area businesses and leave on bulletin boards at grocery stores. Leave your business card with local business owners and managers. If anyone shows interest, you can then set up an appointment and present them with your media kit during the initial meeting.

Develop relationships with fellow Virtual Assistants via associations and forums. Many times established Virtual Assistants will need to subcontract overflow work, and would rather send that work to a Virtual Assistant that they have a relationship with rather than someone they don't know.

Marketing Your Business

Once your business increases and you begin receiving more inquiries and clients from your website and other marketing efforts, don't forget about the alternative methods suggest here. Check out the freelance websites now and again, utilize the skills testing they offer to make sure your skills are still polished and on target with needs of your clients. Continue to participate in online forums and network with fellow Virtual Assistants, the communication and support you will receive from fellow Virtual Assistants is priceless.

Website Basics

Every Virtual Assistant business should have a website to showcase and market their services. Many clients will know you based on visiting your website **_only_**; be sure to make a good first impression! We have outlined the plan to develop your website from start to finish.

Many businesses are using WordPress (wordpress.org) to set up and manage their websites. Using WordPress, is fairly simple once you get started and allows you the freedom to add your own content, make changes easily, and all without the knowledge of html or web design skills.

Plan out your website. Create an outline of your website.

What pages do you want within your site, how will your highlight and represent your service offering?

- Home
- Virtual Assistant Defined
- Benefits of a hiring a Virtual Assistant

Marketing Your Business

- Services Offered
- Fees/Payment Options and Policies
- Code of Ethics/Mission Statement (see e-booklet #5)
- Inquiry Form/Contact Form
- Testimonials
- About (include small bio)
- Certifications
- Press Releases/Media
- Contact

Logo

You will need a high quality logo created for your website as well as for your business. This logo will begin your 'branding' process. The logo should be created not only for viewing on your website, but it should be print ready for business cards and brochures.

If you do not have the skills to create your own logo, there are many graphic designers and logo creation companies that can do it for you.

Layout

Visualize the layout of your website, what colors will you use? What basic theme will be throughout the site – will it be corporate or casual?

Remember when designing your website that it needs to be easy to navigate, a vertical or horizontal menu on every page is ideal.

Google the term 'Virtual Assistant' or 'Virtual Secretary' – to review Virtual Assistant websites to get an idea of what you want for your website. Do not go to these websites and copy their text or their graphics - - just use them as examples for building your own.

There are many website template websites (http://bit.ly/vgalthemes) that provide templates already designed that you can purchase, download and add your information. You still do need to understand basic html and web design to set up your template.

Remember, if you will be using Wordpress and not an html website, you need to search on Wordpress Themes, you will find some free and some professional themes. There are also many free ones listed within Wordpress.

Consider hiring a web designer to create your website for you. Present them with your ideas and outline and they will do the rest.

You will need a webdesign program such as Dreamweaver (http://amzn.to/vgaldw) to work with any html templates that you find. There are also free html programs that you can download and work with to develop your website.

If you will be using WordPress and want something more unique than just free theme you download, Artisteer (http://bit.ly/vgalart) is great software that will allow you to create a Wordpress theme without knowing php or css!

Content

Now that you have your outline, the basic layout and design ready – you need to add content. Take each title/page that you listed in your outline and elaborate on it. Create content for each page. For example, your 'about' page, should include your background and bio. It doesn't have to be too long, but allow your clients to familiarize themselves with you and your experience.

Your website should truly reflect your business. Use other websites as examples but do not copy the content or design – that's illegal.

Register Your Domain Name & Set up Webhosting

Your website is finished, but you still need to put it online – on the web. The first step in doing that is to register your domain name.

When naming your domain, consider your business name, if at all possible your business name and domain should be the same. (see chapter 2 for more details on business and domain names)

After coming up with a great name, get it registered with GoDaddy and set up your hosting, check out Virtual Gal Friday's recommended webhost - HostGator.com (http://bit.ly/qBlLhK)

Uploading via FTP

You have your website completed, and your hosting account all set up. Now, you just need to upload you website to hosting account.

There are many FTP programs available – FTP Commander 8 is a free program and can be found here: http://www.internet-soft.com/ftpcomm.htm

If you feel you need more options, they also offered Pro versions.

Even if you will be using Wordpress, it's still a good idea to have an FTP program, you can do more using FTP than through your webhost file manager.

Keywords, Meta Tags, Submitting to Search Engines

Meta tags are key words to help the search engines find your website. They are placed in the header, in the actual html coding.

Here is a very basic example of what your Meta tags should look like:

    <TITLE>Virtual Assistant </TITLE>
    <META NAME="Keywords" CONTENT="Virtual Assistant, virtual administrative assistant, word processing, spreadsheets, desktop publishing">
    <META NAME="Description" CONTENT="Virtual Assistant Services">
    <META NAME="Author" CONTENT="namehere@virtualassistantexample.com">

The free meta tag generator offered by Submit Express will create your tags for you!

Submit Express - Meta Tags -
http://www.submitexpress.com/metatags.html

Marketing Your Business

They also offer other free tools to optimize your website for the search engines:

- Meta Tag Analyzer
- Keyword Suggestion Tool
- Broken Link Checker
- Free Submission

Don't pay for search engine submissions when you can get what you need for free.

Many webhosting accounts offer free submission services with hosting accounts. Just check within your control panel main menu.

If you will be using Wordpress get the SEO Platinum Pack plugin to manage your MetaTags and SEO. With SEO Platinum Pack, or similar plugins, all the work is done for you in formulating your keywords and tags for each page.

WordPress Set Up

Setting up a website with WordPress is a fairly simple process. All you need to do is open a hosting account, where you can have the Wordpress application installed. Most webhosts now offer free/auto installation of WordPress.

This example shows how to install from a Cpanel, webhosts all offer different control panels, but the features are similar. HostGator.com offers automatic installation when you sign up for a hosting account!

Make Sure you are logged into your webhosting control panel, and click the WordPress icon, or under Software Services, Click on Quick Install.

From the QuickInstall screen, click on Wordpress and then click continue, a new window 'install wordpress' will appear.

Decide the location of your blog - Since you will

Marketing Your Business

be using WordPress for your website, leave the directory box blank. Complete all details required. Click the Install Now! Button.

```
From:     no-reply@designvivacity.virtualgalfriday.com
To:       nancyvgf@gmail.com
Cc:
Subject:  Successful installation

Your new WordPress site has been successfully set up at:

http://designvivacity.virtualgalfriday.com/

You can log in to the administrator account with the following information:

Username: admin
Password: a8EAfWNCq09pWKj8

We hope you enjoy your new site. Thanks!

--The WordPress Team
http://wordpress.org/
```

That's it! You should see a Congratulations message! The system will email you the details with your username and password to the email address provided.

Logging In to Your New Wordpress Website

Once Wordpress is installed, you need to log in to the WordPress administration area from where you can write posts and articles, manage comments, change your theme, etc. To log in the WP admin panel, navigate to the WP login page or directly type the URL in your browser:

http://www.yourdomainname.com/wp-admin/

Posts & Pages in WordPress

In WordPress there are 2 ways to display your content, via pages and posts. Pages are 'static' – these are best for your main website pages like – about us, services, and contact. Posts are where you would add content for your blog.

Wordpress will have a sample page already created, click edit and rename that page to whatever you need it to be for services, about, etc. Create a new blank page for your Blog and name it 'blog' leave it blank. This is where all of your actual blog posts will show up when you add posts. This is why the page should be blank. Click Publish to save the page.

Following the same steps, create another new page and name it Home.

You need to set up WordPress as a website and not just a blog. From the left menu, under Settings, click on 'reading' – then click the button for 'static page' and select post page 'blog' leave the front page blank. This will now make 'home' your home page and blog will show all blog posts.

In the default WordPress installation, there are a couple of themes you can choose from. There are also many websites that offer themes that you can customize to fit your website.

You can find the themes in your WordPress administration area > **Appearance** > **Themes**.

You can change the theme simply by clicking on the desired theme and then **Activate <theme name>**.

If you have purchased or created your own theme, just go to 'upload' to upload and automatically install your theme.

Follow the instructions with your theme for set up of your menus and widgets.

Virtual Assistant Start Up Guide

Chapter 5

Social Media
Social Networking

- Facebook
- Twitter
- Linked In

Social Media & Networking

Getting Connected with Social Media

Social media and social networking are now an integral part of any marketing strategy. Social media is the big picture of how people use the Internet to connect with each other and businesses.

Social networking is using those sites or blogs to actually connect with people (and potential clients) through exchanges such as posting Tweets on Twitter, connecting on LinkedIn, writing on Facebook walls, and posting comments to blogs. It is all about being SOCIAL and building relationships. Offer helpful advice, links to interesting articles or videos that relate to your business.

The use of social media, such as Twitter and Facebook, has become a popular marketing strategy for businesses looking to expand their demographic and gain visibility to potential clients and customers who access these sites daily.

Facebook enables any company to create a profile or Fan Page for your business that potential clients are made aware of through mass invitation. A company sends an invitation to Facebook friends to "become a fan" of their business or product via a customized/personalized message. When someone becomes a fan that information is shared with their network of friends who can see her recent activity each time they log on. *"John just became a fan of Jane Smith Virtual Assistant Services."* For many of their friends, this is enough to make them click over to take a look at your Fan Page, and possibly become a fan as well!

Twitter enables a company to post down to the minute status reports in regards to company activity throughout the day.

A "tweet" for a Virtual Assistant might read: *"What can a VA do for you? - Calendar Management"* and the tweet can also link to your website.

Offering resources and information - not just links to your website - will peak more interest in your tweets and more and more people will start to discuss your information on and off twitter, in online forums, through other social media outlets, or via email. Followers will consider your company a credible source, and any of the products or services offered will also be considered credible.

From a business point of view, the goal of Twitter is networking and reputation building. The key is information – sharing your knowledge with others, and also finding resourceful information posted by others and sharing it with your followers.

When someone comes across an informative resource online they often save it in their 'favorites' or bookmark it. Websites like buzz.com or del.icio.us, are online bookmarking sources where members can save their favorite websites online for others to view. The goal for a business owner, of course, is to have as many end users bookmark their site as possible. When a search engine spider crawls a page and detects a link to their website, the site can increase in relevance. The overall goal is to gain visibility and relevance for your business and your website.

Remember, social media and social networking are parts of the bigger marketing plan for your company. Social media is the practical way to add your Virtual Assistant business into the social networking process that is increasingly becoming more dominant for all businesses to be successful online.

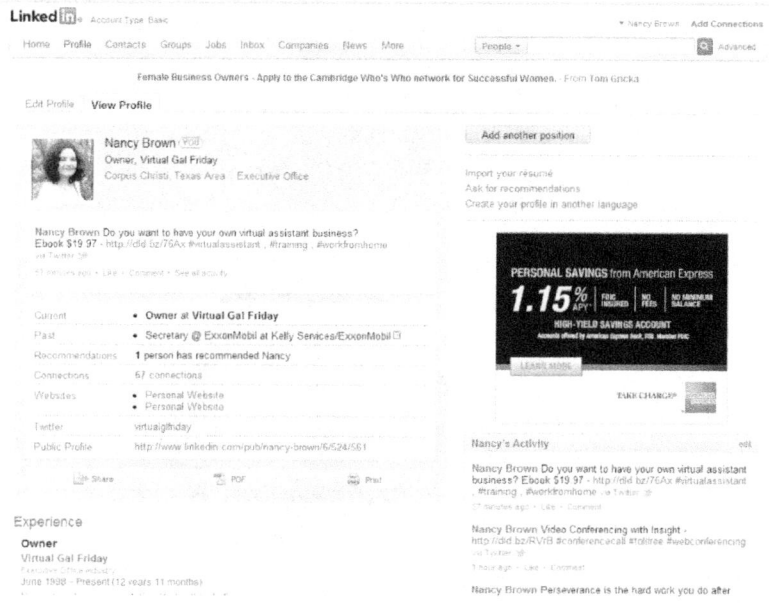

LinkedIn can be described as the formal version of social media. LinkedIn is a business network that can help bridge the gap for job opportunities, networking, job postings and just a great way to connect with industry leaders and potential clients.

A LinkedIn profile can be used as a running resume, so to speak, that can help keep your contacts up to date with current projects or recommendations.

Virtual Assistant Start Up Guide

Virtual Assistant Start Up Guide

Chapter 6

Client Relationships

- Code of Ethics
- Mission Statements
- Client Assessments

Set the Foundation

Starting out on the right foot with a new client is critical to building and maintaining a successful working relationship. During the initial consultation you can set the foundation to a long, successful working relationship by asking insightful questions and being an active listener. This will help you in assessing whether this client will be a good fit for your Virtual Assistant business.

Example Questions:
- What qualities are you looking for in a Virtual Assistant?
- Are you a very 'hands on' person, or are you comfortable letting me run with a project or a new idea?
- How do you spend your time when you are not working?
- Do you have an organized work style, or do you need someone to keep you organized?

Evaluate whether the answers to your questions fit within your characterization of the ideal client for your business. *(we have included a client assessment form with this ebook)*

Trust your instinct

- Are you excited about the possibility of working with this new client?
- Are you nervous?
- Do you like this person?

You can be selective when taking on new clients - do not take on a new client just for the money, even if you feel you need to. The right client will not only be easy to work with, but they could possibly be your next referral source to other like-minded clients. The ideal client will be a natural fit.

Deliver What Your Promise...On Time

Nurture your relationships with your clients by delivering what you promise and keeping your word. It is very important that you strive to meet all deadlines with your clients; this builds your client relationship and shows your clients that they can trust you.

If you can't meet a deadline, let the client know ahead of time so they can make other arrangements if needed. They might be waiting on your work to finish another project, if you don't finish your piece on time that would put your client behind schedule as well. Take responsibility and be honest with your client, do not tell them at the last minute that the project will not be finished on time.

Avoid missing deadlines by allowing yourself ample time to complete a project. Do not tell your client that you can have a project finished in 1 day, if you know it will take 2 or even 3. In fact, you should do the opposite! Let them know you can have a project in 3 days, and when you send them the completed project in

Client Relationships

2 days they will be thrilled with your quick turnaround time.

Don't make promises you know you can't keep, even if a client is pressuring you; you know your capabilities and how long a project will take. Make sure they understand the timeframe upfront. They will appreciate your honesty.

Code of Ethics

Ethical standards play a significant role in all businesses. Clients will not do business with a company they cannot trust, and they definitely won't send referrals to these companies. Consider a code of ethics for your Virtual Assistant business, to show your commitment to honesty, trustworthiness and professionalism. Your code of ethics can be placed on your website, and in your marketing materials.

Client Relationships

Example: Virtual Assistant Code of Ethics

- I will place each client's best interest first
- I will truthfully represent my capabilities.
- I will truthfully represent my skills, and will only offer professional services that I am skilled to provide.
- I will notify potential clients of any conditions that could limit my work performance.
- I will explain the terms and conditions of any client relationship in a signed contract.
- I will honor all contracts, agreements and commitments.
- I will retain precise and satisfactory records of all client work.
- I will protect all confidential information entrusted to me or obtained in the course of any working relationship.
- I will serve as an effective professional representative of my clients when asked to do so, and do everything within my power to protect the interest of my clients at all times.

Mission Statements

What is a Mission Statement?

A mission statement defines what an organization is, why it exists, and its reason for being. Your mission statement should define who your primary clients are, services you provide, and the geographical location in which you operate.

You should be ready to create your mission statement after you have found your business niche (see e-booklet #3). It should capture the spirit of your goals and the ideas that support them. Your mission statement signals what your business is all about to your clients, suppliers and the community.

Create your mission statement by writing down in one or two sentences what the purpose of your Virtual Assistant business is.

Client Relationships

For Example: *"Virtual Assistant 123 Company will provide blog and ezine support services to small business owners worldwide. We will do so by using the newest, most innovative technology at affordable prices."*

You will need to review from time to time and possibly revise your mission statement it to make sure it continues to reflect your goals as your company climates evolves. Simply ask yourself if the statement still correctly describes what you're doing.

Client Relationships

Offer More to Your Clients

Ask your client what more you can do to assist them. Send them an email weekly, maybe even give them a call, and ask them what more you can do.

If you know that your client is traveling to a workshop soon, for example, find out if you can assist with their hotel arrangements, map the city where they will be, make sure their rental car is set up. Be proactive in your assistance with your client.

Make your clients feel like they are your **_ONLY_** client.

Even if you have a full practice, each and every client needs to fill unique and special. You can do this by showing a true interest and passion about their businesses and making yourself available via email, instant messenger or phone when they need you.

Communication is Key

Follow up and communication with current and potential clients is critical to maintaining your client base and building upon it. When you receive a new client inquiry, follow up immediately with a quick email acknowledging receipt and let them know you will follow up with a complete proposal and or phone call to discuss their needs.

Consider setting up a contact form with an auto responder on your website that will email the potential client immediately after they hit the 'submit' button. Be sure to set up your contact form to ask basic questions such as: name, address, email, phone number, timezone, and the services they are interested in. Once a potential client completes your contact form the results are emailed to you. You are then able to prepare for your initial consultation because you have the basic questions answered.

Here is an example auto responder:

"Thank You for your interest in our services. We will contact you via your preferred within XX hours."

When you receive a phone call or email from a current client, respond via their preferred method in a timely fashion. Don't leave them waiting for a returned call or email. Make sure your clients are aware of your daily schedule and response time for responding to emails and phone calls.

Show Appreciation

Show appreciation to your clients. Don't forget holidays, birthdays and other special occasions. Send thank you notes for their ongoing support of your business and for sending referrals to you. Show a genuine personal interest in their life, their goals, and interests.

There are many websites that offer to mail and stamp greeting cards for you, and they even include a personal note!

Offer Additional Services

Encourage your clients to use your full selection of services. This will allow you to continue working with your current clients while you increase your hours and income. You also save money, because you are not always rushing around to find new clients to fill open hours. Your clients also benefit as they give tasks to someone who is capable and trustworthy. The foundation is already there, you just build on it.

Following these guidelines will help you to create a thriving, successful Virtual Assistant business and maintain long-term client relationships.

EXAMPLE
CLIENT ASSESSMENT FORM

During the initial consultation find out as much as you can about this new potential client. Ask questions similar to those below and allow them time to speak, be an active listener. You will learn a lot in a short amount of time and will have the information that you need to decide if they will be a good fit for your Virtual Assistant practice.

Name: _____

Address: _____

City/State/Zip: _____

Phone: _____

Fax: _____

Email: _____

Website URL: _____

1. Tell me about your business. _____

2. What are your business goals? _____

Client Relationships

3. What do you like most about your business? _____

4. Would you consider yourself tech savvy? _____

5. Do you delegate easily? _____

6. Describe your work style: _____

7. Describe your personality: _____

8. Operating system: _____

9. What software do you use? _____

10. Describe your filing system: _____

11. What challenges are you facing now? _____

Client Relationships

12. Do you currently have a Virtual Assistant or in office staff?
   _____

13. What would you say you spend the most time working on?
   _____

14. What tasks do you never seem to have time for?
   _____

15. Have you worked with a VA before?
   _____

16. If yes, how was that experience for you? What was good about it? What didn't work for you?
   _____

17. How many hours per week/month are you needing from a Virtual Assistant?
   _____

Virtual Assistant Start Up Guide

References & Resources

I have included links to the programs and resources I mention throughout the book. The url's that I have included will take you to the exact page that I am referencing. Some of the links look a little strange because they are affiliate links, if you decide to purchase a program or service mentioned in the book, I would appreciate it if you used my affiliate links.

- Microsoft Outlook© - http://amzn.to/oJ9RXm

- Google Apps
  http://www.google.com/apps/intl/en/group/index.html
- Insightly - http://insight.ly/pricing
    Be sure to click the 'add to Google Apps' button for the free version that integrates with Google Apps
- TeamLab.com
- http://www.timeanddate.com/worldclock/
- Skype.com
- YouSendIt.com
- GoDaddy.com
- HostGator.com - The baby plan works great -
- NameBoy.com
- Ryhmer.com
- USPTO.gov - www.uspto.gov/web/trademarks/workflow/start.htm
- Overnight Prints - http://bit.ly/pXYheM
- RingCentral.com
- VANetworking.com
- VirtualAssistantVille.com
- IVAA.org

Virtual Assistant Start Up Guide

- Hourly Worksheet Calculator: http://www.ninafeldman.com/resources/pricing-worksheet
- HireMyMom.com
- Elance.com
- Guru.com

- HTML Templates - http://bit.ly/vgalthemes
- Artisteer - http://bit.ly/vgalart
- Dreamweaver - http://amzn.to/vgaldw

Made in the USA
Coppell, TX
01 April 2022

75855119R00075